ARCHAEOLOGY FOR KIDS
NORTH AMERICA
TOP ARCHAEOLOGICAL DIG SITES AND DISCOVERIES

GUIDE ON ARCHAEOLOGICAL ARTIFACTS
5TH GRADE SOCIAL STUDIES

BABY PROFESSOR
EDUCATION KIDS

Speedy Publishing LLC

40 E. Main St. #1156

Newark, DE 19711

www.speedypublishing.com

Copyright 2017

In this book, we're going to talk about some of the top archaeological dig sites in North America. So, let's get right to it!

CHICHEN ITZA, MEXICO

As the Earth orbits the sun, the shift in its axis separates the year with four different events that mark the seasons:

TEMPLE OF KUKULKAN IN CHICHEN ITZA, MEXICO

The winter solstice, when the day is shorter than the night

The spring equinox, when day and night are the same

The summer solstice, when the day is longer than the night

The autumnal equinox, when day and night are the same once again

CALENDAR

These events separate the year into four seasons with 91 days each.

Although ancient civilizations may not have understood exactly why these changes in day and night happened, they still observed it and were fascinated by it. Some created calendars based on what they saw. These special calendars marked the days for celebrations or so they would know the beginning and ending of the seasons for agriculture.

There are even stone monuments or other sites that were specifically built by ancient people to make note of these events, such as Stonehenge in England or Tikal in Guatemala. Perhaps the most spectacular evidence of this knowledge was found in the ancient civilization of the Mayans.

STONEHENGE

MAYAN PYRAMID

The ancient Mayans built very advanced cities and one such city was Chichén Itzá on the Yucatán Peninsula in the country we know as modern-day Mexico. The Mayans were masters at astronomy and at building complex buildings. Their civilization thrived from about 750 to 1200 AD. When Chichén Itzá was abandoned, it was "swallowed up" by the jungle until archaeologists began excavations in the 19th century.

Perhaps the most amazing building at the site is the temple designed for the serpent god, Kukulkan. The temple has four stepped sides, each with 91 steps for the days in each season. With the top platform, it totals the 365 days in a year. During the two equinoxes, the sun casts a shadow of the edge of the pyramid.

The shadow goes down the edge of the staircase until it connects to the stone sculpture of the snake's head. When the shadow connects to the head, it looks like the giant serpent god is positioned on the side of the temple. What dramatic proof that the Mayans had a masterful knowledge of astronomy! They could even predict eclipses with accuracy.

Sinkhole wells were the only source of water for the city and some of these sinkholes were thought to be passages to the underworld. Victims were sometimes thrown into the sacred sinkholes, called cenotes, to appease the Mayan rain god who supposedly lived in the depths. Archaeologists have dredged up human bones from both adults and children as well as precious jewelry, such as jade, that was worn by the victims or thrown into the cenote to win the god's favor.

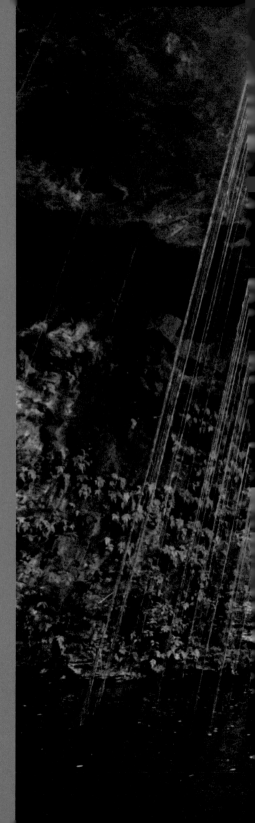

IK-KIL CENOTE, MEXICO

K'INICH JANAAB PAKAL

PALENQUE, MEXICO

Located about 500 miles southeast of Mexico City, the ancient Mayan city of Palenque is at the base of a highland area that overlooks a large section of plains. Archaeologists have found evidence there that the city was inhabited as early as 500 BC. It reached its "golden age" in the 7th Century AD. It was during this golden age that K'inich Janaab Pakal commissioned many amazing buildings that still stand today.

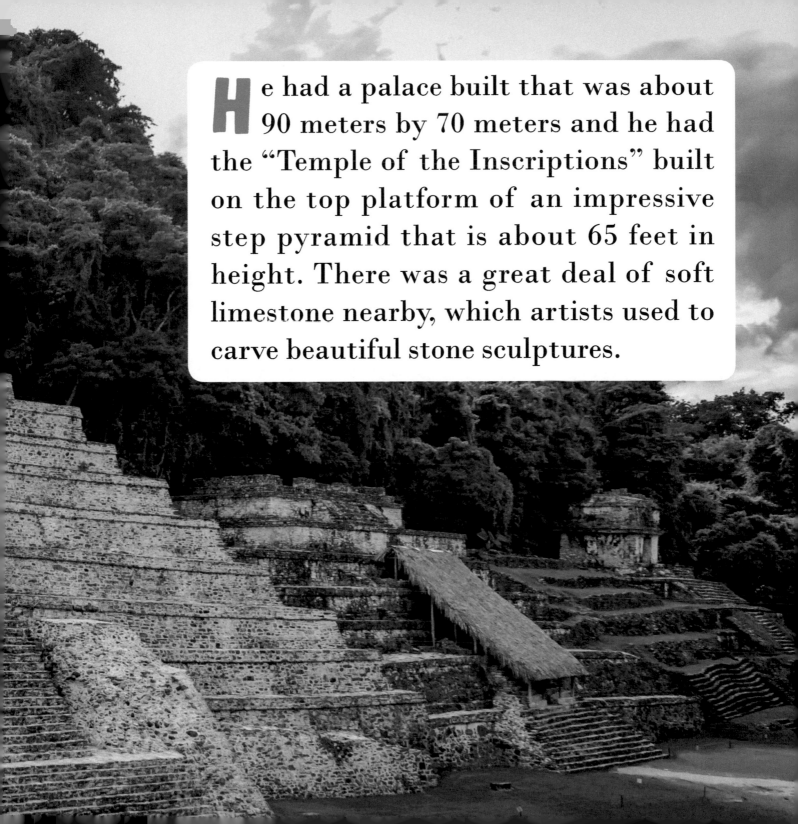

He had a palace built that was about 90 meters by 70 meters and he had the "Temple of the Inscriptions" built on the top platform of an impressive step pyramid that is about 65 feet in height. There was a great deal of soft limestone nearby, which artists used to carve beautiful stone sculptures.

A MAYAN BURIAL MASK

In 1952, archaeologists discovered Pakal's tomb. Inside the tomb was his sarcophagus and many jade objects including a jade mask that the 80-year-old Pakal was wearing when his body was laid to rest. Carvings on his sarcophagus also show a vision of how the king would be born once again with his ancestors, who were depicted as plants. There were also human sacrifices within the tomb that were made to the gods when the king died.

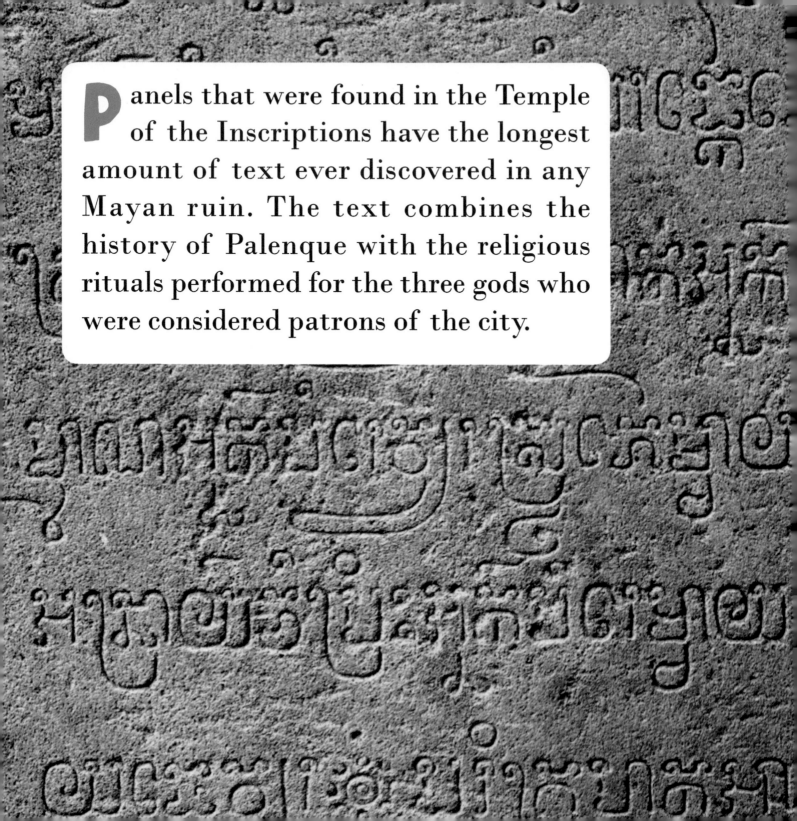

Panels that were found in the Temple of the Inscriptions have the longest amount of text ever discovered in any Mayan ruin. The text combines the history of Palenque with the religious rituals performed for the three gods who were considered patrons of the city.

INSCRIPTIONS AROUND THE TEMPLE

MESA VERDE NATIONAL PARK, UNITED STATES

One day in 1889, a cattle rancher in Colorado by the name of Richard Wetherill and his brothers were looking for some of their stray cattle when they came across a significant find in a plateau area called Mesa Verde. They constructed a quick, makeshift ladder and climbed up to discover amazing abandoned cliff dwellings.

They didn't realize it until much later, but what they had found was the largest group of dwellings built into cliffs that had ever been found. These dwellings had been constructed over 1,000 years before.

GUSTAF NORDENSKIOLD

Wetherill was an amateur archaeologist. He didn't want to see the site plundered as other sites in the area had been in the past. He and his brothers began to carefully gather the pottery and other artifacts there. A wealthy aristocrat by the name of Gustaf Nordenskiold, who also had a keen interest in archaeology, became interested in the site.

He showed the Wetherill brothers how to best preserve many other items, such as ash leftover from fires and trash from the floors. He even saved dried human feces so that later the pieces could be analyzed to determine the diet of the people who lived there.

TREE HOUSE IN MESA VERDE

SUN TEMPLE

Mesa Verde has over 4,700 archaeological sites including Sun Temple, which archaeologists believe the Pueblo Indians used as an astronomical observatory. A recent study done at the location has uncovered that Sun Temple may have been constructed using very precise geometric measurements. Throughout the site, there are also many petroglyphs, which are designs carved into the rocks. In 1906, President Theodore Roosevelt ensured this historic area would be protected when it was designated a national park.

L'ANSE AUX MEADOWS NATIONAL HISTORIC SITE, CANADA

Helge and Anne Ingstad were looking for clues of Viking settlements in Newfoundland, which is a territory of Canada. In 1960, in the small town of L'Anse aux Meadows on Newfoundland's northernmost tip, they met a man by the name of George Decker. He brought them to a site where there were foundations made of sod that resembled Viking longhouses.

VIKING HUT AT L'ANSE AUX MEADOWS

Longhouses were narrow buildings constructed with sod and grassy turf, especially in areas where wood was scarce. More than ten years of archaeological discoveries at the location have proven that the Vikings had a few settlements on the North American continent about 500 years before Columbus came to the New World. They believe that this location was a type of base camp allowing the Vikings a stopping point before they traveled to locations further south.

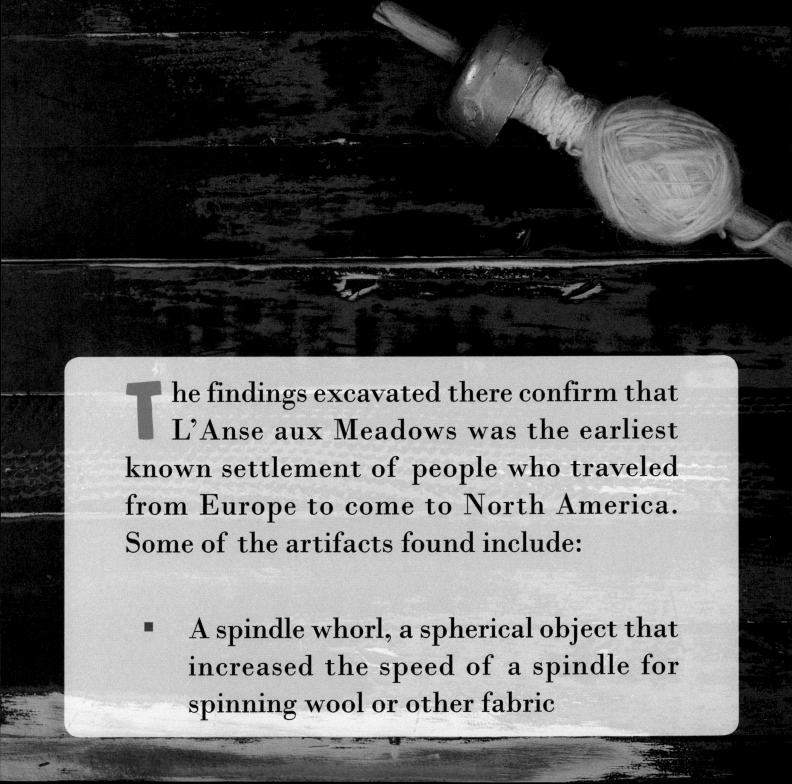

The findings excavated there confirm that L'Anse aux Meadows was the earliest known settlement of people who traveled from Europe to come to North America. Some of the artifacts found include:

- A spindle whorl, a spherical object that increased the speed of a spindle for spinning wool or other fabric

SPINDLE WITH WOOLEN THREAD

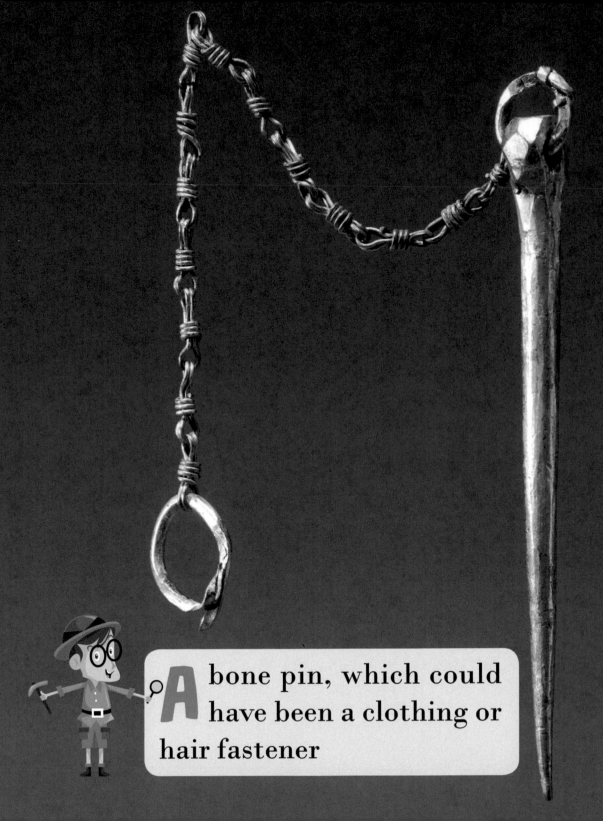

A bone pin, which could have been a clothing or hair fastener

A whetstone, a special stone used for sharpening tools

ron boat rivets, which were used to fasten pieces of a boat together

Carved wood pieces, which were used for decoration

Now that archaeologists have excavated L'Anse aux Meadows for twenty years, they have come to the conclusion that the site was only populated for a few brief years. Perhaps we'll never know why the Vikings didn't build more permanent settlements in North America.

CAHOKIA MOUNDS, UNITED STATES

An ancient Native American Mississippian culture built a very complex society that extended over 4,000 acres in Collinsville, Illinois. This population thrived between the years of 1000 to 1350 AD. They created a huge city of mounds, dwellings, and farms. Monks Mound is enormous. It covers 14 acres and is 1000 feet by 700 feet at its base. Its terraced sides go up 100 feet.

CAHOKIA MOUND

It was possibly a temple and stood as the symbol of the center of the settlement. Another fascinating structure close to Monks Mound is a series of oval pits that were shown to hold wooden posts. An archaeologist by the name of Warren Wittry discovered that when posts were put in place once again, they were in the exact position to make it appear that the sun was rising out of Monks Mound during the equinox.

SUMMARY

North America is the location of many archaeologically significant sites. The ancient Maya people built an advanced civilization in what is now modern-day Mexico. The Vikings from Europe sailed across the Atlantic and reached Newfoundland in Canada five hundred years before Christopher Columbus.

CHRISTOPHER COLUMBUS

In the United States, the Pueblo Indians constructed amazing cliff dwellings in Mesa Verde, Colorado and ancestors of the Native Americans from the Mississippian culture built a complex society in Illinois. Archaeological findings have given us more information about these ancient peoples, but there are still many mysteries to be solved.

Awesome! Now that you've read about some of the interesting archaeological finds in North America you may want to read about amazing ancient civilizations in Africa in the Baby Professor book Archaeology for Kids – Africa –Top Archaeological Dig Sites and Discoveries.

Visit

BABY PROFESSOR
EDUCATION KIDS

www.BabyProfessorBooks.com

to download Free Baby Professor eBooks
and view our catalog of new and exciting
Children's Books

Made in the USA
Middletown, DE
28 December 2020